Grantham
in Focus

GRANTHAM
Journal

at heart publications

First published in 2007 by
At Heart Ltd, 32 Stamford Street, Altrincham,
Cheshire, WA14 1EY

in conjunction with
Grantham Journal, 46 High Street, Grantham, NG31 6NE

Images: Grantham Journal

Text: John Pinchbeck

Cover picture: Barrie Cox

ISBN: 978-1-84547-142-2

Printed and bound by Bell & Bain Ltd., Glasgow

Contents

JOHN PINCHBECK was born in Grantham and brought up in Welham Street when Pidcock's Malting dominated the riverside. A pupil at St Anne's School, Dudley Road, and later the Boys' Central, Sandon Road, he has seen many changes in the town, both good and bad. His family is long associated with the town. His maternal grandfather came to Grantham in 1908, winning a three-year tenancy of the Daily Mail Farm in Little Ponton in a newspaper competition, while John can trace his father's side of the family back as far as 1690, when they had already settled in this area. Many of his family worked for cinema owner John Campbell, others for Richard Hornsby & Son, later Ruston and Hornsby. His grandmother kept a boarding house in Commercial Road, where many of the guests were stars of their day, appearing at the Theatre Royal on George Street. The Pinchbecks have made an impression on the town, even if they may not go down in history, and there is a window in St Wulfram's Church dedicated to them.

John has worked for several county newspapers, including the Grantham Journal, Lincolnshire Echo and Sleaford Standard. He retired as news editor at the Journal earlier this year.

ACKNOWLEDGEMENTS

This book is dedicated to the Journal photographers over the years, including: Ron Dean, Peter Dean, Vic Pell, Max Ewen, Gerry Wright, Jeff Carter and Toby Roberts.

Also thanks to readers who allowed me to use their pictures, including: Shirley Hind, Mike Matsell, Clarry Vickers, Stan Matthews, Jeff Thompson, Malcolm G. Knapp, Peter Nicholls, Keith Harrison, Barrie Cox, Neville Spick, Peter Ball, Ron Crowson, Hazel Tebb, Sue Redmile, Arthur Watchorn, Audrey Vaughan and Kathleen Aspland.

Finally, a big thanks to Richard Adams for his invaluable assistance.

Introduction

IN MANY ways, a time traveller from 150 years ago will still recognise Grantham town centre. Even though few of the buildings predate the Guildhall (1868) the basic shape remains the same.

This book is not just about spotting the difference, but also the similarities. It is strange to see a 1930s picture of St Peter's Hill (west) which immediately is recognisable yet all the buildings have been replaced in the past 40 years.

One of the joys of compiling a book such as this is being presented with a photograph never before seen yet well known. My personal favourite, having been brought up in Welham Street, is of East Street in 1937, which is so familiar – even though it was demolished some years before I was born. Another is Middlemore Yard, which I knew mainly as a car park, although I have often read about the appalling conditions endured by its residents.

Other pictures that have recently come into my possession include wartime BMARCo and Bjorlow's tanneries. Those together with some 1920s Ruston and Hornsby pictures demonstrate what terrible working conditions our forefathers uncomplainingly endured.

Although many of the pictures were taken by Journal photographers, some have been brought in by readers who wanted to share them with a wider audience.

I only hope the reader will enjoy this book as much as I did compiling it.

John Pinchbeck, October 2007

South Parade to North Parade

WE begin with a stroll along Grantham's main street, once a popular route for stagecoaches. This is also a journey through time looking at landmarks, many of which are long gone.

ROY Levicks's garage, North Parade, was a landmark for many years. This picture was taken in the 1960s and it has since been demolished and replaced by flats.

■ MORE than 100 health workers marched through Grantham in 1988 and laid a wreath at the corner shop on North Parade where Prime Minister Margaret Thatcher was born.

Pictured in the foreground are Jean Ward of CoSHE (left), Richard Pitt of the Royal College of Nursing, and Joyce Yates of NUPE, together with Mr Pitt's four-year-old daughter Rachael. They were demanding more Government money for the NHS.

Although the NHS survived, the buildings behind them didn't. The large building is the Blue Bell Inn, on the corner of North Street and Barrowby Road. The building to the left is Leyland Cars dealer, RM Wright. The site of the buildings is now a wider road and part of Asda car park.

■ POLICE measure the road following an accident in Watergate in 1955. Behind is one of the town's Co-op stores, which by then had closed. The tall building on the left was Harrison's, which made and sold osier goods, prams and luggage. These buildings were knocked down to make way for Keymarkets (later Gateway) supermarket.

■ WATERGATE in 1986. This is one road that has changed little over the past 30 years, with Watergate House (right) being the only difference since the demolition of the east side in the 1950s.

■ THE east side of Watergate being demolished in 1964. The wasteland firstly was turned into a garden then a temporary car park. It is still a car park and attempts to redevelop it have been strongly resisted.

■ THE three-quarter acre site on Watergate, which had been used as a temporary car park for 10 years, was put on the market by the owners. The land was originally occupied by shops, which were pulled down in an ambitious development plan. The development had allowed it to be used as a free car park, but the district council decided to buy the land and start charging for parking.

■ WHIPPLE'S haberdashery, Watergate, in 1897, the year of Queen Victoria's Diamond Jubilee. The shop was destroyed by fire in 1916.

■ DEMOLITION of shops on the corner of Vine Street and Watergate went ahead in February 1960 to widen the road and make way for a modern development, Watergate House. Sharpley's shop had already been demolished to widen Watergate.

■ HIGH Street in 1962, before Boots, which had another branch on London Road, moved to its new location. Next door is Timothy White and Taylor's pharmacy and houseware shop. The building for sale is the former Central cinema.

■ GRANTHAM Round Table were out collecting for charity in 1960 on the High Street.

Woolworth was still being built. The store moved from Market Place. Next door is the Journal's new office, on the site of the previous one. The collector at the front is Fred Goodliff, before he became editor of the Grantham Journal.

■ HIGH Street in 1938. What brave motorist would dare drive down the middle of the road now? Indeed, even a cyclist takes his life in his hands. The stationer's is W G Harrison.

■ AN oak tree is planted in front of the Guildhall, St Peter's Hill, in 2004, looking strangely like the classic war photograph of planting the Stars and Stripes on Iwo Jima. Improvements to the green caused much consternation when the public saw trees being felled, but they soon appreciated the improvements.

■ LITTLE has changed at the Guildhall since it was built in 1868, although this picture taken in the 19th Century, before the trees matured on the green, reveals more than most.

Notice the add-ons, which include the homes of the Chief Constable and the Inspector of Weights and Measures.

■ QUEEN Victoria's Diamond Jubilee in 1897 and the building on the site of what was to become the Picture House. The building to the right became the Rainbow Cafe.

■ ST Peter's Hill in 1924. Only the Guildhall survived development which created Grantham Public Library and later the exit from the bus station.

■ Mr White's piano shop, St Peter's Hill, around 1910. It later became White & Sentance.

■ THE Westminster Bank prepares to open for business in about 1958, next door to its present site. White & Sentance was a well-established music shop with another branch in Wharf Road.

■ THE new NatWest Bank in 1987 with the old premises still next door.

■ GRANTHAM'S jobless took to the streets in January 1972 to demonstrate against the country's unemployment. They were addressed by TUC General Secretary Len Murray.

These women and children outside the Guildhall were against both the Conservative Government and its Education Minister Margaret Thatcher who famously earned the name 'Milk Snatcher' after cancelling the free milk for schools scheme.

■ THE old sorting office in Bath Street behind the post office was demolished. A former Army hut, it had been there since 1917, replacing the one in the Market Place which proved too small for the number of parcels being delivered to the troops stationed at Harrowby and Belton military camps. The replacement in 1969 was no larger but the layout was far superior.

■ THE toilet block and shop at the old bus station, St Peter's Hill, was pulled down to make way for the £1.5 million district council building in 1986.

■ GRANTHAM Concert Band provided the music for the St George's Day parade in 1976. They are marching along London Road where there are familiar shop names from the past including the Co-op, Fashioncarry, the Long Bar and Watkins.

■ LONDON Road in 1986, which still shows the legendary Long Bar. Co-op Travel was still part of the main store and Graham Watkin was still selling pork pies.

■ THE lock-up shops on London Road, next to the Nag's Head, were already looking tatty in 1986. Ten years later they were boarded up and became the town's principal eyesore until they were demolished to make way for Leonard Audus House.

Market Place and Westgate

ONCE the main shopping area of the town, the buildings, apart from the shop frontages, have hardly changed here since Georgian times.

WIDE Westgate during the visit of Harold Macmillan in 1959. The large building is Neales, one of the town's main furniture shops at the time. The buildings have changed little.

■ THERE were many complaints in 1978 that stallholders on Grantham Market didn't clean up afterwards. Little has changed.

■ WHARF Road railway bridge in 1977. On the right is the former Bridge Hotel which had been Vacu-Lug Social Club before moving to George Street. It was demolished to make way for a roundabout.

■ THIS crypt was discovered under a building in Butchers Row on April 26, 1888. Unfortunately this fine example of Medieval craftsmanship was not preserved, due to the cellar being filled with concrete.

■ THE Chequers Inn, Butchers Row, in the 1880s before it was demolished and a pub of the same name built on the site.

■ BUTCHERS Row at the turn of the 20th Century. The larger building has been variously Dixon & Parker and Aitch.

■ GRANTHAM cattle market on a wet day in 2003. It was closed due to foot and mouth disease and never reopened. It was demolished and Augustine Retail Park built on the site.

Castlegate area

ONE of the oldest parts of town and the heart of the conservation area. This is a beautiful part of town but it once saw some of the most appalling conditions.

CASTLEGATE in the early 20th Century. The Victoria Nursing Association is on the right. It has since been incorporated into an insurance office. The buildings on the left now belong to accountants Duncan & Toplis.

■ CASTLEGATE House, once the Conservative Club before it moved to nearby Middlemore Yard into purpose-built premises. It is now a residential home.

■ MIDDLEMORE Yard in the 1930s. The houses were cleared and now form part of the Conservative Club car park. It looks amicable enough but these were among the worst housing conditions in Grantham.

■ EMPTY cottages at the top of East Street in June 1937 just before they were demolished. The tall building on the right is the rear of the Theatre Royal (also known as the Empire Theatre when it showed films). The stage door was in East Street. In the distance is Pidcock's Maltings in Welham Street. The two road-sweepers going down the hill are on their way to the borough yard at the bottom of East Street, where they would have kept their barrows and tipped their sweepings.

■ EAST Street in March 1938 after a start had been made to demolish the cottages at the top of the hill. The street was originally called Well Lane but its name was changed during the late 19th Century. The tall chimney which has been exposed is the electricity generator on Agnes Street.

■ THE Central Methodist Church in the 1880s. Little has changed, although the garden was still intact in those days and had yet to be sacrificed to make way for a car park.

■ THE old Spiritualist Church on the corner of Finkin Street and Elmer Street South, boarded up in 1985 due to vandalism. The name English Dogs scrawled on the wall was that of a Grantham-based punk band which had some success in the indie charts.

■ THE ceiling rose over the spiral staircase in Granta House, Finkin Street, now occupied by Brown & Co. The building was originally the headquarters for Grantham Philosophical Institute in the early 1800s.

■ THE boardroom in Granta House, Finkin Street, occupied by Brown & Co. Originally the centre of the floor was open, with library shelves around the circular wall. Natural light comes from a copula. The building was originally erected as the headquarters for Grantham Philosophical Institute in the early 1800s.

Little Gonerby

ONCE a separate parish, Little Gonerby lies north of Brook Street. It was once home to some of the area's most dreadful slums.

THE old gymnasium in Brook Street, one the buildings that was to make way for the Empire Garage in 1952. It had many uses in its time, including a theatre and a seed warehouse.

■ THE Empire Garage, which was build on the site of the former Gymnasium in 1952 by Lou Musson. It remained in the motor trade until the new millennium when the site became an extension to The King's School.

■ EMPIRE Garage was eventually taken over by Safe Petroleum and when that closed, was purchased by The King's School for an extension.

■ MILLARDS Place at the rear of Vere Court in 1934. The buildings in the foreground are outdoor toilets which were shared by the residents.

■ VERE Court was demolished in about 1937. It was a notorious area off Broad Street which ran behind Alfred Robert's corner shop. The houses were condemned and even had earth floors.

■ HOUSES in James Street being demolished in 1937. The street crossed Vere Street and together they formed the island which later became Premier Court. These streets were the view from a young Margaret Thatcher's bedroom. At the end of the street is White House, in Brownlow Street.

■ MOWBECK Cottages, Union Street, in 1937.

Wharf Road area

THE north side of Wharf Road was mainly demolished in the 1980s but the south side was left virtually intact. There have been some interesting developments on the streets to the south.

WOODBINE Cottages, Wharf Road, had already been demolished in 1982, leaving the wall of Cheshire's pharmacy exposed. In the distance is Les Davy's plumbing supplies business.

■ WHARF Road in 1986. Burton's shoe shop, which had been there for decades would soon close, although Brewer and Allen saw in the millennium.

THE slipper baths, Wharf Road, in 1982 awaiting demolition. The road to the right is Bath Street. To the left is the Baptist Church, the only building that remained after 1985.

■ BATH Street in 1982, showing the Post Office sorting office and Billiard Hall on the right. In the distance is the Granada which by then was a bingo hall with little future.

■ As the Welby Street area is cleared for development in 1982, all that remains is the Granada Bingo Hall (former Cinema). The building remained after the development of the Isaac Newton Centre and Morrisons.

■ THE Maltings before restoration. It had been exposed in 1982 by the demolition of Jackson's garage. For many years its future was in doubt, with becoming a night club, arts centre or demolition among the options. Instead it was restored in 1989 as prestige offices.

■ JACKSON'S garage on the corner of Wharf Road and Wide Westgate. It was demolished for the Wharf Road roundabout. Behind it is the maltings. The photograph was taken from Station Road (West).

■ MOST of the industrial building in Brewery Hill belonged to Mowbray's brewery, which had closed in the early 1960s following a series of takeovers. The building on the right became Kingdom Hall, the church of the Jehovah's Witnesses. The picture was taken around 1984.

■ COMMERCIAL Road in 1982. Notice the boot scrapers by the side of each door. The building just before the white wall is the Primitive Methodist Chapel, which later became the Electric Club.

■ GEORGE Pollard's Shop in Norton Street, taken in 1984. The decrepit shop supplied nearly every part the amateur car mechanic could wish for and at a very good price.

It was pulled down in about 2004 and developed into flats. The building housing Grantham Organs was once the Norton Arms while the building opposite was the Army Recruiting Office.

■ RAILWAY Terrace in 1984, which has seen many improvements and developments over the past few years. The building on the left was once the Layton Arms pub.

■ WILLIAM Street, linking Norton Street and Grantley Street, in 1984.

■ ELTON Street showing Pollards automotive shop on the corner. The shop and area around it have been developed since the picture was taken in 1984.

■ GRANTLEY Street in 1982 at its junction with Wharf Road. On the left is the Golden Fleece pub, which became Churchill's and a clothing shop was on the other side, once Dawsons the butchers.

■ GRANTLEY Street and William Street in 1984.

■ LAUNDER Terrace, seen here from the rear, suffered badly in a gale which ripped through the town in 1976.

■ THE Big Top Circus came to town in April 1961, and elephants marched through Grantham from the railway station to the circus in Wyndham Park. The policeman is guiding them down Station Road (West).

Swinegate area

ONE of the town's oldest streets, and most likely Grantham's original high street. This is another area that kept its beauty and charm well hidden for many years, and it was not until demolition loomed that many of its secrets were revealed.

THIS archway was the entrance to Artichoke Yard, which was one of the casualties of the pre-war slum clearance programme.

■ BEHIND the wall was Artichoke Yard which was demolished some 70 years ago.

■ EXPOSING the timbers of Artichoke House was a big improvement for the former pub, but the replacement building on the left never fitted in with the rest of the street.

■ THE Blue Pig, from Swinegate, in 1932, as the rendering was being removed to expose the timbers beneath.

■ JOHNSON'S Yard, Swinegate, in 1938.

■ THE Blue Pig, from Vine Street, next door to Read's Laundry in 1937 after the timbers had been revealed.

■ QUEEN Victoria's Golden Jubilee in 1887 was an excuse to decorate the town and have a party. This picture shows the east side of Swinegate, near Church Trees, which has changed little.

■ LITTLE has changed in Vine Street over the centuries, although Read's Laundry, which was still there when this picture was taken in the 1950s, later moved to a purpose-built laundry on Harlaxton Road.

■ TAXI proprietor Chris Bland with his Ford Zephyr in 1965 waiting on Swinegate for a bride and groom to come out of St Wulfram's Church. With him is John Daybell of Denton. In the background is Burton's Garage and the Co-op's New Street store is in the far distance. Artichoke House behind him has not yet had its timbers revealed.

Welby Street area

WELBY Street and Stanton Street were at the heart of major bulldozing in the early 1980s to make way for the Isaac Newton Centre.

WELBY Street in 1982. Men wearing neither safety harnesses nor helmets demolished the remaining shops to make way for the Isaac Newton Centre.

■ THE Plough Inn, Welby Street, together with the shop next door, await demolition in 1982.

■ WELBY Street had been partly demolished in 1982, exposing the school. The car is emerging from Greenwood's Row car park, roughly where the footpath leading to Welby Street is now.

■ JOHN Lee and Son, Welby Street, being demolished in 1981. Welby Street School can just be seen to the left and The Maltings is in the distance. The building on the right was also part of the Lee complex, with Hands Yard running down the side, partly in a tunnel created by the buildings along the side of the Granada. Lee's was what would now be called a 'recycling company' where rabbit pelts, which would later be used to trim hats, were left hanging to dry in the windows.

■ GREENWOOD'S car park with the Journal offices and Woolworth's in the background. This part of Welby Street has changed little since this photograph was taken in 1984, apart from the road, which was swallowed up by the Isaac Newton Centre development.

■ RUTLAND Street (left) and Stanton Street (right) had been demolished for the Isaac Newton development in 1983. The building on the far left was The Maltings, which was later converted into smart offices.

■ HANDS Yard, which ran from High Street to Welby Street. These cottages were demolished in the 1930s to make way for the State (later Granada) cinema.

■ LAST days of the Granada in 1988. A hole had been knocked in the sidewall off Bath Street for demolition contractors to get their equipment inside.

■ THIS once insalubrious site was turned into Horse and Jockey Yard in 2005. The wall was removed, a small park laid out and, to complete the transformation, the yard was renamed in deference to a pub that had stood on the site until the 1950s. The building to the left is the Journal and to the right is Boots.

Around town

THIS collection of pictures of other areas of town do not fit into any specific area, but are certainly worthy of inclusion.

MEMBERS of Grantham Civic Trust's clear-it-out task force and local youngsters with some of the rubbish taken out of the Grantham Canal near Earlesfield Lane Bridge in 1969.

■ THERE was a big clean-up of the Grantham Canal in 1970 with tonnes of rubbish pulled out between the wharf and Earlesfield Lane Bridge.

■ THE dedication of the Church of the Epiphany, Earlesfield, by the Bishop of Grantham the Rt Rev Dennis Hawker in 1975. In the centre is Vicar of Grantham, Canon Graham Sansbury.

■ PROTESTORS concerned about dumping nuclear waste at Fulbeck by Nirex made a stand when a Government minister was at Dysart Road. William Waldegrave was there to open the Woodland Trust offices in 1986. The charity was taking over the former R H Neal's offices.

■ VOLUNTEERS working on the Church of the Ascension, Edinburgh Road, in 1954, took a well-deserved tea break.

■ THE prefabs in Belton Avenue received a facelift in 1983, their first since they were built, when they were given brick skins and tiles. They had been built just after the Second World War.

■ THIS house on the corner of Goldsmith Road was one of hundreds damaged by a 100mph whirlwind, some 50 metres wide, which swept through the town in 1977 leaving a trail of destruction.

■ MAYOR of Grantham, Ivan Dawson, digs the first sod for the foundations of the Canterbury Close sheltered housing complex, Queensway.

■ PENSIONS Corner, so called because the Ministry of Pensions once had an office there. The people are meeting their children out of Harrowby Infants School, New Beacon Road, and were accused of causing road chaos in 1991.

■ HARROWBY Road in 1912 with the new St Anne's Church on the right. Apart from the clothes of passersby, and the tree in the foreground which has long gone, this photograph could have been taken yesterday.

■ BOURNE Cottages, Inner Street, in 1934 just before demolition.

■ THE Catholic Parade celebrating the Feast of Corpus Christi leaves Albion Terrace for Brook Street in June 1961. Apart from a lack of parked vehicles, very little has changed in 40 years.

■ THIS German-made Okal House was built in 72 hours in 1988 by developer Bocock. It never caught on and no more were built. This show house became Gifts Hospice, then a children's day nursery.

■ THE southern part of town seen from the tower of St Vincent's in 2000. In the distance, left, is Moray Firth's malt silo, Springfield Road. In the centre is London Road industrial estate, formerly Ruston and Hornsby.

■ SPRINGFIELD Road in 1999 with the allotments to the left protected by barbed wire. This was one road that developers could only improve.

■ TWO 60ft mobile cranes, each worth £15,000 raised sixteen 26-tonne concrete beams into place to form the parapets for the Harlaxton Road flyover in 1960.

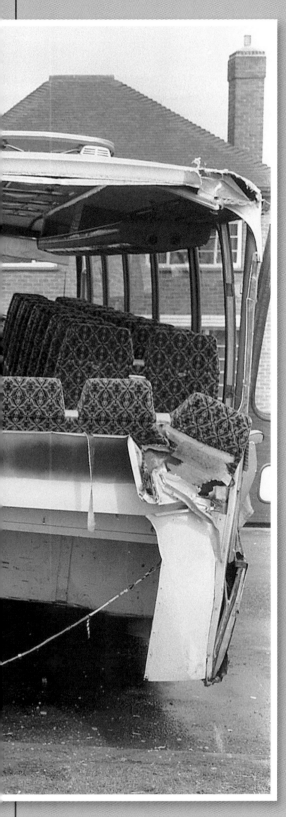

■ SEVEN people were taken to hospital when a bus travelling from Birmingham to Skegness skidded into a lamppost and demolished a garden wall. It happened on Harlaxton Road in 1976, near the end of Kitty Briggs Lane.

■ ROADWORKS are nothing new in Grantham – and they are still as bad as ever. This shows Dysart Road bridge over the A1 closed for seven weeks in 1976, forcing a detour for anyone wishing to go to Barrowby.

■ BARROWBY Gate in 1981 when residents were concerned it would become a shortcut for lorries heading for the A52. On the left is Valley Road with Durham Close further up the hill.

■ SWALLOW'S Mill, also known as Spittlegate Mill, in 1962. The main house later became a night club, then Vacu-Lug's offices. In the 1990s a developer took over the site and with conversions and new-builds made it a prestige housing development.

■ DYSART Road railway bridge being demolished in 1971, 120 years after it was built for the Ambergate Railway. The white buildings are Chandler's Fuels and the factory in the background is Coles Cranes.

■ ST ANNE'S Church, Harrowby Road, held a pet service in October 1968 to celebrate the feast of St Francis of Assisi. The church was built in 1907, next door to the cemetery, to replace a church further down and across the road known as the 'Tin Tabernacle'. At the back of the picture is the vicar, the Rev A. G. B. Parsons with his whippets and RSPCA inspector Tony Booth.

■ THIS house, which was occupied by the council nursery, and the bus shelter attached were demolished for a new development after this picture was taken in 1984. The Manthorpe Road property was said to be haunted.

Focus on the railway

GRANTHAM became a major railway town as soon as the first lines were laid. The first was the Ambergate Railway, opened in 1850, of which little remains; and the East Coast Main Line was completed in 1852 with very little ceremony. It was with GNR and later LNER that the locomotive department known as 'The Loco' prospered with more than 1,000 men working there.

■ A GOODS train passing the old granary at Grantham railway station in 1964. This locomotive would have once hauled passenger trains but by now steam power was on its way out. So too was the granary, which has long been demolished and is now part of the railway car park.

■ THE railway yards were closing down in 1964 and the coaling tower, which used to fill the tenders of the locomotives, was redundant. It stood on the site later occupied by the canning factory, Springfield Road. In the distance you can see the shop on the corner of Victoria Street. Peter Nicholls, of Gorse Rise, Grantham, was at the scene when the concrete structure was blown up. He said: "It was done in secret for safety reasons. They didn't want a crowd. But at 8am, when it was due to be blown up, it was thick fog. The contractors had to wait until 2pm for it to clear." Then, with the press of a button, the tower, which had been a landmark since 1937, came crashing down.

■ LOOKING rather tatty, this once proud locomotive is demoted to pulling a goods train in 1964. Prior to the Second World War it would have been in LNER green livery and cleaned every day.

■ A GOODS train waits in Grantham station in 1964. Notice the old footbridge, which has since been replaced.

■ A LOCOMOTIVE takes on water at Grantham station in 1964. By then it was already becoming an endangered species. Note the old-fashioned signals.

■ DRIVER Lofty Shields and fireman Phil Cunnington are captured in this 1955 photograph at Grantham station. These were days when Grantham was an important railway town and hundreds of people still worked at the Loco. The name of this locomotive was Silurian.

■ IN 1962, engine no 63982 was laid to rest at F. C. Larkinson's canalside scrapyard for dismantling. The picture shows 19-year-old Clarry Vickers with a welding torch beginning to cut the steel into sections to be melted down at Scunthorpe. This was promised to be the first of many locos to be dismantled by the scrap yard. In the event, it was the only one. The scrap yard was taken over by TW Ward of Sheffield.

■ A PICTURESQUE view in 1982 taken from Spittlegate Hill railway bridge. The building on the left is Read's canning factory which closed in 2006, while on the right is Aveling Barford, now Jackson Building Supplies.

■ THE Flying Scotsman emerges from the northern end of Peascliffe in 1983. There was no shortage of admirers trespassing to watch the historic locomotive.

■ THE approach to Grantham Railway Station, 1985

■ THE ticket office of Grantham Railway Station following a facelift in 1985.

■ RAILWAY Station buffet and paper stand, 1985. Originally a WH Smith kiosk, the newspaper sales were later transferred to the cafe.

■ GRANTHAM station platform 1985. It was originally built in about 1852.

Focus on shops

HERE we have a selection of shops which are no longer with us and, in some cases, trades which have completely disappeared. There were several tobacconists in the town as well as toy shops and butchers which hung their goods on display outside the shop.

NEALE'S began mainly as a china shop and, on several occasions, beast escaping from the nearby cattle market found their way in there. It moved more and more into furniture and took on toys at Christmas. It was taken over by Times Furnishers but went into decline. The building became a nightclub upstairs and a wine seller on the ground floor.

■ D. E. CHANDLER'S shop, Westgate, in 1951. The doorway was soon filled in to improve the windows. The company claimed it could supply everything from a cotter pin to a combine harvester.

■ THE latest in fireplaces and kitchenware from D. E. Chandler's Westgate shop in 1951. Notice the small mangles in the foreground.

■ H. WELBOURN & Son's tobacconist shop in Westgate is pictured here in 1982. The shop was previously Mayfield, but Mr Welbourn moved there when his North Street business was demolished to make way for Premier Court. To the right is Houghton's the jewellers, still there 25 years on.

■ ARTHUR Watchorn senior in the 1930s outside the shop on the corner of Westgate and Guildhall Street. The business was taken over by his son, also Arthur, but when he retired it kept the name for a spell before becoming Nelsons.

■ THE Market Place in 1985. Only Mark Jarvis remains. The shops either end, together with the floors above the entire block, became Notions Antiques. The white patch on the taller building used to read 'YMCA', which had moved there from Wharf Road.

■ BUDGET shoe shop, Jonathan James, was one of many businesses to occupy this building after Woolworth's moved out in about 1960. It eventually became a pub, first Hogshead then Gravity. Paddy McBride ran the fish and chip shop when this picture was taken in 1983. Paddy was never short of ideas for publicity, such as hiring a security firm to take a sack of potatoes to his bank when the price of potatoes went through the roof.

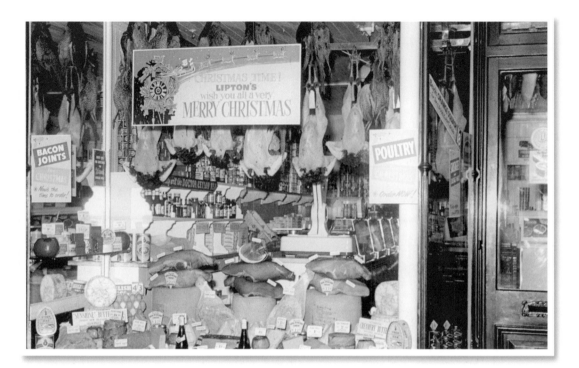

■ THERE were special treats on offer for Christmas Day in Lipton's High Street store window as food became plentiful in the late 1950s. Frozen food wasn't the norm then as few people owned fridges and even fewer had freezers. Instead, most meat, poultry, fruit and vegetables were fresh, while anything out of season was tinned.

■ GRANTHAM'S first town centre supermarket, Tesco, opened on St Peter's Hill in the 1960s, although the Co-op on Princess Drive was already in business.. This picture was taken just before it opened its doors for the first time.

■ THE central mall of the Isaac Newton Centre began to take shape in 1983. This is looking towards Welby Street.

■ A FASHION show inside the newly opened Isaac Newton Centre in 1984.

■ THE cash desk in Beever's High Street drapery when it closed in 1984.

■ ARTHUR Chambers was a leading fashion store in Grantham for many years, with an attractive staircase inside. It was looking very sorry in 1986 when this picture was taken, but found a new lease of life as Yorkshire Bank.

■ THESE two ladies worked at the Co-op shoe department in St Catherine's Road in the 1930s. The railings disappeared during the Second World War. The door is now the entrance to the Tollemache Inn.

■ GRANTHAM Co-op in 1972 before it became Great Nottingham Co-op. It closed in the mid-1990s and became a pub and fitness centre initially.

■ PLAMORE Sport, managed by former Grantham FC manager and Norwich City and Peterborough United star Terry Bly moved from Wharf Road to Westgate in 1982. Before that the shop was owned by 'Baggie' Bates who ran an electrical shop also selling cycles and fishing gear. Originally a chapel it was bulldozed to make way for the new bus station.

■ WHIPPLES Garage in 1908-1910. It later moved to the Watergate site, which it occupied until the 1980s. It was opposite the George Hotel and later became tailor George Mills, and then Burtons. Notice the cars in the first floor showroom.

■ VINE Street in 1986. Willoughby's flower shop eventually became a café, and Go Sing takeaway became a printers, but Grantham Beauty Clinic lives on.

■ CHARITY'S leather goods shop was a rare survivor in Wharf Road in 1982. Peter Wallwork's furniture shop next door had already gone.

■ THE Windsor Fish Restaurant was modernised in 1967. To the right was the Blue Horse, which later also became a fish and chip shop. Pawson Plumbers was on the left.

■ SAFEWAY supermarket nears completion on the former London Road football and cricket ground in 1991.

■ SAFEWAY exterior, London Road, in 2004, before being taken over first by Morrisons and then by Sainsbury's.

■ THE corner shop on North Parade and Broad Street, steam-cleaned and re-roofed to become an upmarket restaurant. Rodney Cloke was the man behind it. It became the Premier Restaurant, after other names like Maggie's Café, Blue Angel and Right Bite were rejected. The Premier had seating for 48 covers. The reception was laid out like a shop of the 1930s.

■ CONNOR'S shop on Harrowby Road, near the Methodist Church. This was taken in the 1960s but the shop closed many years ago and was demolished.

■ THE southern end of London Road in 1986 with Nova Fashions split by a butcher's shop. The double-fronted shop was a video rental shop of which there were about a dozen in town at the time.

Focus on education

LIFE for Grantham's schoolboys and girls has changed tremendously over the years. Many of the old schools, including the Wesleyan and Welby Street have fallen by the wayside, while others such as Spitalgate and St Anne's have carried their names to newer premises.

BUILT in 1858 – the foundation stone is incorporated in the Isaac Newton Centre – Welby Street School was demolished in 1983 as the area fell to the developers. It wasn't until then that the school became wholly visible to the public.

■ TUCKED away surrounded by houses, a cinema and John Lee's rag and skin factory, Welby Street School ran for about 80 years. It closed in 1940 when pupil numbers had fallen so low it was considered too expensive to run. Spitalgate School pupils moved there for a short spell to avoid the bombing, although they stayed for less than a year.

It never reopened and was later used for storage. In 1930 it had a major overhaul with central heating and electric lighting introduced. It raised the money mainly from whist drives. The picture taken in 1932 confirms the area was not a wealthy one.

■ THE old Wesleyan School, Wharf Road, pictured here in 1984. It had closed many years earlier and the building was used as the central school meals kitchens. It was eventually demolished to make way for flats.

■ PUPILS at Harrowby
Infant School enjoying
the traditional maypole
dance in 1968.

■ PARENTS walking to
Isaac Newton School
and Ambergate School
had to brave filthy
conditions on their way.
The children never
seemed to complain
though.

■ THE teaching staff at St Anne's School, Dudley Road, in May 1962, in the days when classes-sizes could be 50 pupils or more.

Pictured from the left (back row): Winifred Cooper, Audrey Vaughan, Beryl Lilley and Audry Brown; (front row): Mrs White, Mrs Harris (head) and Mrs Mabel Harrison.

■ WYNDHAM Park day nursery opened its £350,000 centre in 1997. It was Grantham's oldest nursery, launched during the Second World War for the mothers working in munitions factories.

■ KESTEVEN and Grantham Girls' School in 1960.

■ THE girls at Kesteven and Grantham Girls' School in 1958 listen as headmistress Miss Gillies addresses them on their annual prize-giving in the Drill Hall, Sandon Road.

■ PRINCE Philip visited Grantham schools in May 1973 to inspect the success of his Duke of Edinburgh award scheme. He arrived at St Hugh's Comprehensive School by Wessex helicopter. At The King's School, he watched this display by the girl gymnasts.

■ SPRINGFIELD County Secondary School opened its new hall and gymnasium in July 1961, a bargain at £20,000. Inside it was fully equipped with changing rooms and showers, and offered comfortable seating for up to 350 people. These lads are pictured taking the seating inside.

■ WALTON Girls' High School a few days after it opened in 1966. Originally the Girls' Central School, the old school building dating from the 1920s just didn't come up to scratch. Work began in 1964 in a field off Kitty Briggs Lane and two years later the four-storey structure was opened. The Girls' Central had been dark, with outside toilets across the playground from the main building, so the 300 pupils were delighted with their new light and airy premises. Incidentally, the old school had only two headteachers in its history, Miss Jabet and Miss Nina Hewitt.

■ EARLESFIELD Secondary Modern School (later St Hugh's) nears completion in February 1960 at a total cost of £180,000.

■ BOYS at St Wulfram's Secondary Modern School (later Grantham Church School) enjoy life in the gymnasium in 1962. These lads were attempting to move the components of a cannon over a 'ravine' without losing any of them.

■ STUDENTS learn typing at Grantham College in 1981, using what was then the latest technology. The heavy, manual typewriters now seem very primitive.

■ SOUTH Witham School in the 1950s.

■ BILLINGBOROUGH School in 1890.

■ THE teacher on the right of this picture of Foston School, in 1889, has the definitive 'wasp-waist'. Unfortunately we do not have her name. The vicar is the Rev Michael Edward Mills and Percy Dickinson is the tallest lad on the back row.

Focus on the hospital

GRANTHAM Hospital was first opened in 1976 with seven beds each for men and women. Within 10 years, water was pouring through the roof when it was discovered the timbers were poor and the tiles were not laid properly. Despite millions of pounds being spent at the site there have since been many threats of closure, leading to several protests by the people of the town.

GRANTHAM Hospital taken from the maternity wing in 1985. Work is in progress to build a new car park.

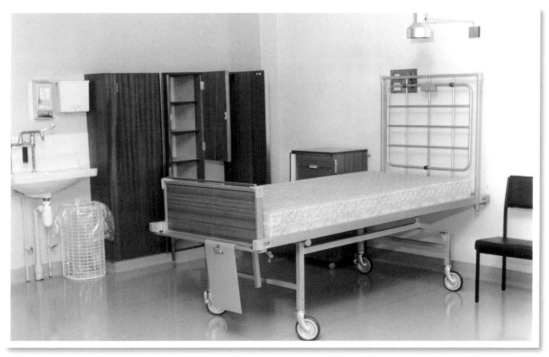

■ INSIDE Grantham Hospital's new maternity wing in 1972. Everything then was state of the art, but the department has had a chequered existence ever since.

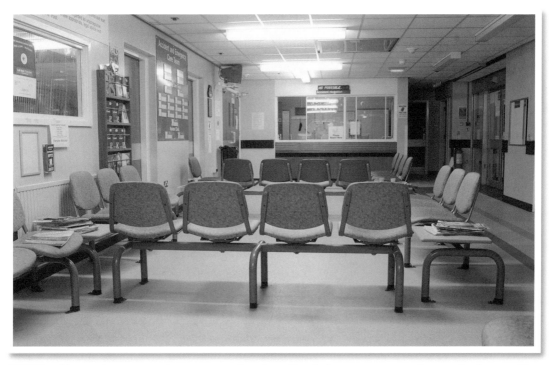

■ THE accident and emergency department at Grantham Hospital at 2.30am on a quiet morning in 2004. The future of the department hung in the balance for years to come.

Focus on work

FOR many years, Grantham's economy was based on engineering but, following a decline which began in the 1960s, the town's employment moved to service industries and food processing.

RUSTON and Hornsby fitting shop in 1928. Health and safety had a low priority in those days when there was no shortage of engineers in town.

■ HEAVY Machine shop at Ruston and Hornsby in 1928.

■ RUSTON and Hornsby's fitting shop working on horizontal oil engines around 1928.

■ THE final traces of Ruston and Hornsby's empire were to be swept away in 1988. Top End, North Parade, which included a fitting shop and packing shop had been used by Aveling Barford, but was surplus to its requirements. It was rebuilt for a builders merchants and later a retail park was added.

■ THE old drawing office of Ruston and Hornsby, Station Road East, is demolished in 1998. It had more recently been home to wedding gown makers Bridal Fashions, also known as Hilary Morgan, for several years until the company moved to Springfield Industrial Estate. The picture is taken from London Road, with St John's Church in the background.

■ THE old Journal building made way for its replacement in 1959. Greenwood's Row and its car park were yet to be built.

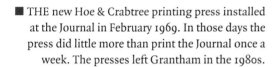

■ THE new Hoe & Crabtree printing press installed at the Journal in February 1969. In those days the press did little more than print the Journal once a week. The presses left Grantham in the 1980s.

■ EDDISON Plant in the 1960s. The offices behind are on a rather sparse looking Harlaxton Road. They later became the magistrates and county courts. At the top right of the picture are the Springfield Road allotments.

■ FREDA, the Eddison Plant-owned steam roller, outside the company's Harlaxton Road headquarters in 1969. From left to right are Tom Morgan, area manager David Leverett, and Mac Pooley.

■ THE main factory at Bjorlow's tanneries, Earlesfield Lane. No trace remains other than the former offices on the other side of the road. It is now Hollis Road Industrial Estate.

THE gloomy interior of Bjorlow's tannery.

■ MP Joe Godber (right) watches Doug Musson operate at Bjorlow's tannery, Earlesfield Lane. With them is works manager Hempton.

■ BJORLOW'S tannery in the 1970s shortly before it closed. It was built alongside the canal on the site of its predecessor, Shaw's. The bridge to the left carried Earlesfield Lane.

■ THE recruitment of men into the armed forces during the Second World War left a void at the town's munitions factories. To fill it, women were employed. This young woman added the feminine touch by having flowers at her workbench at BMARCo.

■ WOMEN working on munitions at BMARCo during the Second World War. The internal brick walls were to reduce the blast from any falling bombs.

■ LADIES busy in the munitions department at BMARCo in the 1960s.

■ WITHAM Contours, which had taken over the Harlaxton Road premises of Reads Laundry, had itself closed in 2003. The building was demolished to make way for a trade park.

■ DEMOLITION had begun at Witham Contours on Harlaxton Road in 2004.

■ IMPRESS Packaging in 2004. Originally built as American Can in 1969 on the former railway marshalling yards off Springfield Road, it mainly provided cans for the pet food industry. It had several names, including Pecheney, as it changed ownership. It closed as Impress in 2006 and was demolished to make way for a new housing development the following year.

■ INSIDE Pechiney (later Impress) can-making plant in 1994.

■ PRIME Minister Sir Alec Douglas Home visited Aveling Barford in 1963. He is seen here inspecting a mechanical shovel.

■ INSIDE Pechiney's factory in 1994.

■ AVELING Barford had taken over the South Parade works of Ruston and Hornsby in the early 1970s for its spares department. It became a retail park for stores including Aldi, Dunelm Mill and Jackson Building Supplies.

■ AVELING Barford's South Parade site in 1977. It was formerly part of the Ruston and Hornsby complex, and later Jackson Building Supplies. The houses in the background are in Stamford Street.

■ THE storage area of Aveling Barford Houghton Road in 1977.

■ IN 1947, these former Army buildings were used by Kontak Manufacturing (now Parker Hannifin) near Belton Park Golf Club. The unit in the centre was the work's canteen and social club.

■ SEVEN-year-old Neil Taylor's dream came true thanks to major employer Aveling Barford. In 1976 his sister Carole failed to get his dream fulfilled by TV personality Jimmy Savile on his show Jim'll Fix It. So she wrote to the company which stepped in to allow Neil, of Cornwall Close, Grantham, to ride in a giant 50-tonne Centaur dumper, made at the Houghton Road plant. He was taken for a ride by demonstrator Max Whittaker at British Leyland's testing grounds at Ropsley.

Neil's opinion of the ride: "It was very fast and noisy. I want to be a dumper driver when I grow up." The picture shows Neil and Max with the giant dumper.

■ PART of the roof of Coles Cranes canteen blew off and was scattered along Dysart Road during gales in January 1976. The building has since been demolished and the site taken over by Autumn Park.

■ THE massive steel warehouse being built on Dysart Road for John Lee Steel Services (later Corus). It was pulled down in 2006 for the Matalan/Homebase development.

■ THE Mayor Councillor Herbert Harris paid a visit to the GPO telephone exchange, which at the time was situated over the Post Office, St Peter's Hill. It was Christmas 1964.

Focus on play

IN the 1980s, Grantham won the 'Golden Yawn Award', a prize voted for by Radio 1 listeners, thus citing it as the most boring town in Britain because there was nothing to do. The following pages explode this myth.

THE Mid-Lent Fair in 1952, showing Joe Ling's men putting up the waltzers in the Market Place. The picture was taken from the YMCA (now Notions Antiques).

■ DODGEMS being assembled for the Mid-Lent Fair outside the Blue Bull, Wide Westgate, in March 1952.

■ THE opening of Grantham's Mid-Lent Fair in March 1953 when the Mayor would traditionally read the proclamation from the steps of the Market Cross. There was always a good turnout to watch the ceremony in those days.

■ VISITORS to Grantham Mid-Lent Fair in 1951 enjoy the caterpillar ride. A canopy on the left enclosed each car at top speed and all the lights went out.

■ ONE of the attractions at the Mid-Lent Fair in 1983. The riders stood around the side as it sped round, relying on centrifugal force to keep them in place. Ogden's, incidentally, was a garden shop on the corner of Market Place and Conduit Lane, before garden centres became popular.

■ THE Granada Cinema towards the end of its normal life in 1972. It closed less than a month after this picture was taken. It became a bingo hall with occasional big shows but was finally demolished in 1988, together with the Guildhall (formerly Railway) Tavern.

■ WOLF cubs sports day at the Boys' Central School ground, Sandon Road in 1957. The Mayor is Fred Foster.

■ CUBS marching along London Road in 1976 for the St George's Day parade.

■ GRANTHAM Choral Society was backed by the Manchester Mozart Orchestra for its performance of Faure's Requiem and Vaughan Williams' Sea Symphony in 1976. The society was formed in 1963 to celebrate Grantham's Quincentenary year. The concert, as usual, was held in St Wulfram's Church.

■ GRANTHAM Singers, formed in the early 1950s, are seen here rehearsing at the Central School on Rushcliffe Road, in 1988. It was the final year as conductor for Rodney Dawkins who had taken over the baton in 1967 as a 19-year-old music student.

■ BELTON Jazz Festival 1983, which starred world class saxophonists Red Holloway, left, and the legendary Sonny Stitt.

■ BELTON Jazz Festival in 1983. The enthusiastic audience in the marquee in the stately home's grounds enjoyed top American bee-bop stars Sonny Stitt and Red Holloway. Others on the bill included jazz dancer Will Gaines, the Best of British and Five-a-Slide.

■ CHILDREN at the popular Hill View Adventure Playground had painted a mural on the concrete wall which bounded their play area. The year is 1981.

■ A FOLK Festival held at Aveling Barford in 1988 was a washout with artistes outnumbering visitors. The inclement weather had a lot to do with it. Even so, the event made a very modest profit thanks to sponsorship.

■ A CHILDREN'S parade through Earlesfield estate was preceded by a barbecue and fancy dress party at Hill View Adventure Playground off Derwent Road in 1976, shortly before it was officially opened by Peter Tomlinson of ATV's Tiswas. The event was organised by play leader Lars Hallengren with more than 100 children taking part.

■ HILL View Adventure Playground off Derwent Road with Warmington Hall in the background. These lads are assembled for a five-a-side football competition. The site of Hill View workhouse was closed by the county council and eventually redeveloped.

■ BMARCo's Social Club, which once rang to the sound of Grantham's top groups, awaits demolition in February 1999. Throughout the 1960s and 1970s it had been one of the town's premier entertainment spots.

■ THE Newton Fraction Road Race which ran through Grantham in 1988. It had just turned from Castlegate into Avenue Road.

■ WORK gets under way on the £1million leisure centre in Union Street in 1981, which incorporated the indoor swimming pool. The complex was demolished some 10 years later to make way for an Asda superstore and a new leisure centre was built off Trent Road.

■ THE Quincentenary indoor swimming pool on Union Street in 1972, at Grantham Swimming Club's annual gala.

■ THE indoor swimming pool, Union Street, was evacuated in July 1974 following the escape of chlorine gas.

■ THE London Road football ground in February 1978. Play was abandoned before Grantham FC's opponents even set off. The background buildings on the right, including the tower, are in Brewery Hill.

■ GRANTHAM FC's dressing rooms at the old London Road ground in 1988. Originally stables for the Blue Horse next door, they were soon to be demolished to make way for a Safeway supermarket.

Focus on pubs

PUBS come and go and many change their names. The Granby became Eden, The Blue Man became the Maltshovels and the Blue Ram reverted to the King's Arms. At one time there was something like 140 pubs in Grantham, and that's just the ones with names. In the 19th Century, many became 'Blue' pubs but only the Pig and the Bull remain.

THE White Hart, High Street, before improvements in 1957. The pub closed in the mid-1980s and the site developed as a McDonald's fast food restaurant.

■ THE Manners Arms, London Road, in about 1938. It was pulled down in the new millennium and Pizza Hut was built on the site. Across the road is Ruston and Hornsby's factory, but the buildings were destroyed in a bombing raid in the early 1940s.

■ THE Black Dog in 1985.

■ THE Gatehouse (later the Playhouse) in Watergate, taken in 1987. The building was formerly Collard's ironmongers which sold everything from screws ("what thread sir?") to shotguns. The building was erected in about 1760 and the new pub included a 150-year-old waterwheel inside.

■ THE Crown and Anchor pub, Swinegate, just a couple of doors from the Blue Pig. It closed as a pub in 1936.

■ THE former Durham Ox, on the corner of Welby Street and Wharf Road, is demolished in 1983 to make way for the Isaac Newton Centre. It ceased to be a pub in 1961.

■ WHAT was left of Welby Street in 1982. The tall building is the Plough Inn, which was about to be demolished as part of the town centre developments. It had been closed since 1958.

■ BARCLAYS Bank in the 1960s, on the corner of High Street and Guildhall Street. In the 1990s the bank moved to smaller, more modern premises while this building became a pub called the Goose at the Bank.

■ THE Fox Inn, by the side of the A1 at Colsterworth in the 1950s before it became 'Tudorised'.

■ THE Blue Boy, Foston, which closed in the 1960s.

■ THE Blue
Cow, South
Witham.

Focus from the air

AERIAL photographs have a fascination of their own, and can put a whole new perspective on the town, even if they were only taken yesterday.

THE central building with a white roof in this 2001 photograph is Asda with the railway line running behind. The white road on the left is Westgate. Premier Court is in the lower centre and the new buildings to the right are Spire View. Westgate runs vertically on the left joining Harlaxton Road at the railway bridge.

■ THIS view of Grantham in 2001 is easy once you get your bearings. The church near centre top is the cemetery chapel. Running upwards is Wharf Road and St Catherine's Road. Lower left of centre is Morrisons and the multi-storey car park.

■ A BIRD'S eye view of Grantham from the west in 2001. Bottom right are buildings on Springfield Park, formerly BMARC, while lower centre is Moray Firth Maltings. Harlaxton Road runs upwards from bottom.

■ RUNNING upwards from the centre is Brook Street towards the square that is Premier Court. Just above the cockpit is the old leisure centre in Union Street. On the extreme upper left Westgate meets Harlaxton Road at the railway bridge. The year is 1995.

■ GRANTHAM from the air in 2001. At the top is Asda superstore, bottom left is the Fine Fare store and indoor car park. Moving right we see Crown House.

■ AN interesting town centre picture from 1935. The Market Place has changed little, other than every shop had blinds back then. In the bottom left are buildings in Conduit Lane which have now disappeared, in fact the area looks more developed than it is now. Note the vicarage, surrounded by trees, has Victorian wings added to the Georgian building. These were demolished in the late 1950s.

■ NOT strictly an aerial photograph, although it was taken from 50 metres up St Wulfram's church tower in 1968. The street running along the left is Castlegate while the building midway up the right is Elm House, Elmer Street North. In the foreground is the north side of Bluegate although many of the buildings above it have since been demolished.

■ THE railways go their separate ways, running bottom to left for Nottingham and straight up for Yorkshire and Scotland. The foreground buildings, pictured in 1988, are those of Foot and Padley's, which had recently taken over the Wolsey factory on the trading estate at Gonerby Hill. In the top of the picture you can see Arnoldfield House. Housing development had only just begun.

■ FENLAND Foods factory (bottom right) from the air in 1988. The houses are off Shaw Road, with Swingbridge Road running parallel (right). Above the housing estate are Texas Homecare and Miller Bros (later Ritz Bingo). Top right is Spitalgate School.

■ ST Hugh's School from the air in 1962, with the Meres playing fields in the foreground, later developed for the stadium and sports centre.

■ THE year is 1918. The square in the centre is the town's football ground before the club moved to London Road to join the cricket club. The newly-built Huntingtower Road School is surrounded by fields along what was known as Workhouse Lane and later Station Approach. Running left to right is Harlaxton Road.

■ AN interesting picture from 1918 shows Harlaxton Airfield. A few buildings remain on Gorse Lane.

■ THIS is a reconnaissance photograph taken in 1918. The square to the left is The King's School Quad.

■ THE A1 Grantham bypass being built in 1960. The old road is meandering right towards Grantham from Little Ponton while the route of the new road is to the left. There has yet to be any development at Spittlegate Level.

Focus on the villages

HERE we leave the town and have a look at some of the fascinating villages we have surrounding Grantham.

HOLY Trinity Church roof repairs in 2004 were due to cost £70,000. Allington church warden John Swallow is pictured with the church in the background. He said: "When they stripped the lead from the roof, the beams were in worse condition than first thought. We had to replace at least two beams over the nave."

■ THE Great North Road (A1) running through Colsterworth in 1910.

■ CROXTON Kerrial at the turn of the 19th Century. It has seen plenty of development since.

■ FOSTON Dovecote circa 1910. Built in medieval times, it was constructed of mud bonded with straw and pebbles. It was bulldozed in 1960 to make way for the A1 Foston bypass.

■ FEEDING the fowls at Foston in the early 1900s.

■ CLEANING out the crew yard at Bagguley's Farm, Foston, circa 1950.

■ JOURNAL photographer Gerry Wright took the opportunity to produce this unusual photograph of Bottesford. It shows a workman replacing the weather vane at St Mary's Church, Bottesford, in 1998.

■ HARLAXTON Manor in 1962, when it was in the hands of the Jesuit Order.

■ HARLAXTON quarry train in 1976, shortly before it closed.

■ THESE children were keen to meet the postman on this day in the 1950s, because for one of them there were birthday cards. It was taken at Hungerton by the postman.

■ INGOLDSBY as seen from the church tower in the early 1900s.

■ POSTMAN Bernard Bullock is pictured here on his motorcycle combination at Oasby post office. He is chatting to Miss Johnson, the village postmaster's daughter.

■ THE new A1 Grantham bypass is open to traffic in 1960 at Little Ponton. Some critics at the time said there was not enough traffic to justify it.

■ RIPPINGALE in the 1920s.

■ ROPSLEY in the early 1900s.

■ ROPSLEY in the early 1900s.

■ THE Manor restaurant, Long Bennington, was closed and demolished in 1988. It made way for a housing development.

■ THE National Coal Board was looking at the Vale of Belvoir as a lucrative new source in 1976. This test rig was operating between Denton and Casthorpe.

■ ALL that was left of West Willoughby Hall in 1963 after demolition men moved in with explosives. The former stately home, just before Ancaster, had been commandeered during the war and ended its days as a fertiliser factory. Only the stables remain today.

■ VOLUNTEERS from South Witham planting roses in the churchyard in November 1937. They are, from left to right, Mr Messam, Len Ford, George Farnsworth, the Rev Ronayne, Arthur Dickinson, William Holt, Bill Adams, Sid Ford and Joff Batty.

■ GOOSEBERRY Hill, South Witham, in the 1900s.

■ HIGH Street, South Witham, in the 1900s.

■ WATER Lane, South Witham, in the early 1900s.

■ E M CRAVEN'S shop at South Witham more than a century ago.